MONKEYS

Susan Canizares
Pamela Chanko

Scholastic Inc.

NEW YORK • TORONTO • LONDON • AUCKLAND • SYDNEY

Acknowledgments

Science Consultants: Patrick R. Thomas, Ph.D., Bronx Zoo/Wildlife Conservation Park; Glenn Phillips, The New York Botanical Garden; **Literacy Specialist:** Maria Utefsky, Reading Recovery Coordinator, District 2, New York City

Design: MKR Design, Inc.

Photo Research: Barbara Scott

Endnotes: Susan Russell

Photographs: Cover: Wolfgang Kaehler; p. 1: John Guistina/The Wildlife Collection; p. 2: Michael Fogden/DRK Photo; pp. 3 & 4: John Guistina/The Wildlife Collection; pp. 5 & 6: Jack Swenson/The Wildlife Collection; p. 7: Luiz Claudio Marigo/Peter Arnold, Inc.; pp. 8 & 9: Peter Welmann/Animals, Animals; p. 10: John Guistina/The Wildlife Collection; p. 11: Wolfgang Kaehler; p. 12: Jack Swenson/The Wildlife Collection.

Library of Congress Cataloging-in-Publication Data
Chanko, Pamela, 1968-
Monkeys / Pamela Chanko, Susan Canizares.
p. cm. -- (Science emergent readers)
"Scholastic early childhood."
Includes index.
Summary: Photographs and simple text explore the daily activities of monkeys in the Amazon rainforest.
ISBN 0-590-76964-2 (pbk.: alk. paper)
1. Monkeys--Juvenile literature. [1. Monkeys.]
I. Canizares, Susan, 1960- . II. Title. III. Series.
QL737.P9C455 1998
599.8--dc21   97-34203
                                                               CIP AC

5   6   7   8   9   10   03   02   01   00   99   98

What do monkeys do?

Monkeys climb.

Monkeys swing.

Monkeys hang.

Monkeys jump.

Monkeys ride.

Monkeys rest.

Monkeys screech.

Monkeys stare.

Monkeys hug.

Monkeys kiss.

Monkeys monkey around!

Monkeys

Monkeys represent two of the groups of mammals that make up the order of primates. One of the things that sets monkeys apart is their amazing abilitiy to live in trees (mostly in the tropical regions around the equator). What helps these creatures stay aloft is the way they climb. They use their hands and feet to grasp the branches. Most other animals climb by digging their claws into the bark of the tree the way a bear would. Monkeys' special grasping ability has made their way of living very successful.

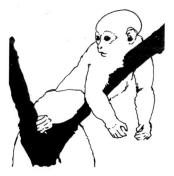

Tails are also very important to monkeys. Most monkeys' tails are long and supple and can wrap around branches, holding on as tight as another hand. This helps them balance and swing through the trees with great speed and agility. Their tails are often strong enough to carry their entire weight, allowing their arms to stay free for reaching. Their back legs are very strong, too, and help them jump farther, faster, and higher.

Monkeys and their close cousins, the apes, live in complex social groups. Each of the groups has a definite territory where it lives, gathers food, and feels most relaxed and secure. One of the ways monkeys define their territory is with sound. Different groups signal their ownership with different sounds; some by screeching, some by howling, and others by whooping. Sound making is also a way to warn other monkeys of nearby predators.

Baby monkeys ride on their mothers' bodies. The infant monkey can, and must, cling to its mother's front or back so that her arms and legs are free for climbing, foraging, moving through the trees, and even escaping from danger if necessary. All of this holding on strengthens the young monkey's grasp, an ability it will need to use all its life.

Mother monkeys hug their babies close. Babies are born singly, and newborn monkeys are as helpless as newborn humans. They must stay with their mothers for food and protection. But they mature much faster than humans. After just a few weeks they begin to eat like other monkeys, gathering leaves and fruit. By the time they are about a year old, they are weaned and ready to go out on their own.

Touching is a vital means of communication for monkeys. Family groups show their comfort with each other by playing, holding, and grooming one another. Monkeys form bonds of friendship and affection just as humans do. This close contact helps keep the group together and feeling secure.